RECIPES & IDEAS

# LIGHTING

RECIPES & IDEAS

# LIGHTING
Simple Solutions for the Home

by Sally Storey

CHRONICLE BOOKS
SAN FRANCISCO

First published in the United States in 2000 by Chronicle Books

Editorial Director: Jane O'Shea
Consultant Art Director: Helen Lewis
Project Editor: Nicki Marshall
Consultant Editor: Eleanor Van Zandt
Design Assistant: Sarah Emery
Production: Julie Hadingham
Special Photography: Tom Stewart
Picture Researcher: Nadine Bazar

Library of Congress Cataloging-in-Publication Data
Storey, Sally.
Lighting: recipes & ideas: simple solutions for the home / by Sally
Storey.
    p.  cm.
ISBN 0-81182716-X
1. Lighting, Architectural and decorative. 2. Interior decoration. I. Title.
    NK2115.5.L5X76 2000              99-37296
    747'.92—dc21                     CIP

Printed and bound in Hong Kong

Interior design and layout by Quadrille Publishing
Cover design by Amy Knapp

Distributed in Canada by Raincoast Books
8680 Cambie Street
Vancouver, British Columbia V6P 6M9

10 9 8 7 6 5 4 3 2 1

Chronicle Books
85 Second Street
San Francisco, California 94105

www.chroniclebooks.com

*To Lucca, Cazalla, and Alexander*

*Page 1:* Decorative patterns with a traditional lantern.

*Page 2:* Wall-mounted uplights provide the general light in
the room. The wire track system has pendant
spotlights over the table and small, directional spotlights at either end. The wires carry the current and
are powered by a remote transformer.

*Page 5:* A narrow beam spotlight provides a central focus
to the dining table and allows a wash of light over
the place settings.

*Publisher's note*
Throughout the book, measurements are given in both
standard and metric. When planning a lighting scheme
or when buying fixtures, use either all standard or all metric
measurements, as the two are not necessarily
interchangeable.

# contents

introduction

Lighting is one of the most difficult design concepts to understand. Light is all around us, but we cannot touch or feel it, and yet it is responsible for all that we see; without light we perceive nothing. Interior designers use color swatches or samples to demonstrate a creative effect and to help make decisions, but it is difficult to prepare a sample board of "lighting effects." The way light is used will, in fact, change the way that we see everything.

The potential of light has long been exploited in the theater where the powerful combinations of light and shade, tone and color, are used to create the mood for each set and direct our focus toward important characters or objects around the stage. The same detailed understanding of lighting is fundamental to photography. There is no reason why domestic lighting should not create the same powerful effects as in artistic disciplines.

## Light and shade

Good lighting stems from an understanding of the balance between light and shade. In simple terms, lighting is the presentation of space. If used skillfully, it provides the final invisible touches to your design. Artificial light thrown onto the surfaces of a room from different heights and angles will change its apparent dimensions. It can emphasize height, structure, and materials, and become almost an architectural element itself.

Whether your interior is traditional or contemporary, the lighting will set the mood. But good lighting should not really be noticed: it should enhance your interiors and provide a wonderfully creative environment without *obviously* doing so. To the unpracticed eye, it is only bad lighting that is noticed. This may be because it is too bright or too dark, because the light sources glare into your eyes, or because it draws attention to the wrong elements of a room.

For many people, the traditional central pendant is the main source of light—lighting in all directions but with little focus or direction. This type of lighting is unexciting and rarely fulfills a room's potential; combined with table lamps and other light sources, however, it can be effective.

1 This halo effect is created by a floating canvas panel surrounded by fluorescent bulbs with blue filters to color the light.

2 The play of sunlight, shining through the grid at an angle, creates wonderful speckled patterns of light across the wall.

3 Natural light filters through louvered shutters, and combines with the warmth of a table lamp for a soft, daytime scheme.

The creative potential of modern lighting is discussed here, along with how to use its flexibility to best effect. Light can be manipulated to dim, brighten, obscure, and highlight, and to create plays of shadow and color; it can transform the atmosphere of the room just as theatrical lighting transforms a scene. This is the great advantage of lighting over all other design aspects. Good lighting design means flexibility; it enables a family kitchen used for the preparation of food, for example, to be transformed at the flick of a switch from a bright, functional space into an intimate dining area for a party.

## Lighting techniques

It is important to understand from the beginning that good lighting is usually made up of a number of effects. Just as an interior decorator layers his or her textures and paint finishes, a lighting designer will use a variety of different lighting techniques in each room to achieve an overall result. It is by balancing the intensity of the various effects that lighting moods are created.

This book gives an introduction to the use of this evocative element of decoration. First, it gives a description of the basic tools and techniques. It then goes through a

house room by room, considering the lighting require-ments of each as well as any special problems they may pose. None of the suggested ideas is, however, the only solution, as interior lighting offers endless potential and variety. The suggestions are for inspiration and to demon-strate a palette of lighting effects, so that you can decorate with light just as an artist uses color. With this in mind, it is essential to understand some of the powerful tools available to the lighting designer. These can be summarized as the light source itself and the method of how the light is manip-ulated within a room or garden.

① Surrounded by open space and woodland, this house has little need for privacy, and so natural light can flood in. During winter evenings, candles along the window ledge and a log fire add softness and warmth, but the outside view is the focus.

② If a garden feature, such as a tree or fountain, is lit from the outside, a focus is produced beyond the glass to create a feeling of spaciousness. This helps to eliminate the problem of a window's appearing like a mirror after dark.

③ An incandescent tube has been recessed into the ceiling to give a wash of light down the wall, making it appear to glow.

1 Recessed low-voltage uplights, close to the wall, create narrow shafts of light down the wall and reflected light from the ceiling above. Downlights recessed into the ceiling provide both downward light and a wall-wash effect, due to their proximity to the wall.

2 This soft incandescent uplight-effect can be achieved with either a mini track or tubes, to provide definition around the ceiling. The warmth of the light contrasts with the bright white-ness of the cabinets.

There are six main lighting tools: downlighting, uplighting, wall-washing, feature lighting, color, and control. These fall within the overall divisions of general lighting, task lighting, and feature lighting.

Uplighting, downlighting, and wall-washing can be used to create general lighting if several light sources are positioned around the room. Used individually, they can provide feature lighting by creating focus on flowers or a painting, for example, or even highlighting an architectural feature. Similarly, when used individually they can provide useful task lights, such as those needed for reading or cooking. The elements of feature and task lighting overlay the general lighting to create an effective scheme for each room.

*Downlighting*

Of the modern approaches to lighting, downlighting is possibly the most conventional. It is direct and generally energy-efficient, as it concentrates the lighting in the specific area where it is required. Downlights, usually recessed into the ceiling, form a three-dimensional cone, or arc, of light which will vary in size depending on the beam angle. If you concentrate downlights within the center of a room, the cones of light will not spill onto the wall and create unwanted "arcs" of light.

Downlighting is often used imaginatively, but excessive use of it in the center can make a room appear gloomy, as the floor is well-lit while the walls and ceiling remain in shadow. In these instances, some light on the walls may be desired. This is why it is important to understand lighting design in three dimensions and the effect of an arc of light across a wall. You should position your downlights not so as to create a symmetrical pattern of light on the ceiling, but to achieve the best effects on your walls: the closeness of your downlight to the wall and the beam width of your bulb (see page 98) will affect the pattern of light on the wall. A downlight with a wide beam will, when positioned close to a wall, make the arc of light begin higher. Downlighting tends to work best in rooms with high ceilings, as the beams of light created overlap, and the light becomes more diffuse.

*Uplighting*

Uplighting enhances a sense of height, making a room appear more spacious than it is. The principal purpose of uplights is to direct light up at the ceiling, which acts as a reflector. If your ceiling is light in color, this will provide a very diffuse, general light while creating a sense of space. Uplights offer more flexibility than downlights: they can be wall-mounted or free-standing, high- or low-level, and are available with a wide number of different bulb (lamp) types.

Ideally, uplights should be positioned in pairs to give a sense of symmetry. Due to the intensity of their light, halogen uplights at the side of a room can create sharp lines across the wall, so you must ensure that this line does not cut across a picture or piece of furniture. If the lights are positioned in front of a window or mirror, this line of light will not be noticed, and against a dark wall the beam shape could become a feature in itself. Tall, free-standing uplights come in many different styles to suit every interior. These lend themselves especially well to control with a dimmer switch (see page 90), which can be installed at little cost. A floor-standing, drum-shaped uplight can be used with a low-voltage bulb as an excellent way of lighting dark corners of a room.

*Wall-washing*

This is accomplished with ceiling-mounted fixtures which direct their light evenly across a wall and can provide part of the general lighting. Unlike downlights and uplights, wall-washers emphasize the vertical surfaces in your room, and are especially useful in enlarging the perceived width of a room. As with other techniques, the brighter the color of the wall, the greater the amount of reflected light.

Wall-washers are also particularly useful for emphasizing wall texture, pictures, or cabinets. Similar in appearance to downlights, they will need either to be adjustable or to have an additional reflector (see page 98) to direct the light. The positioning of wall-washers is critical to ensure an even distribution of light. For best effect, fixtures usually need to be 28–40 in. (70–100 cm.) apart, and distance from the wall depends on the type of fixture and the ceiling height.

## Feature lighting

This can be used to highlight chosen features in a room, while hiding less significant details. Feature lighting works best when the light source itself remains hidden: your eye is naturally drawn to the brightest point within a room, and if the bulb or fixture were visible this would be the focus. A recessed fixture that spotlights a picture, or a narrow-beam uplight that highlights a column or arch, works well. Low-voltage miniature directional sources are the most versatile solution. You need to pay special attention to the position of the lamps and use the right beam width for the object being lit. To highlight a wall-mounted feature, the light should normally be between the viewer and the wall.

You need to create the right intensity of light to make the most of each object, and not bleed out any color by overlighting or bleaching it. It is recommended that the feature lighting within a room be controlled separately from the general light to maximize the effect (see page 90).

## Color

Rather than colored filters or lamps as in photography, "color" to the lighting designer is the selection of a light source to emphasize the true color of what is being lit. Different light sources have different color temperatures. For example, an incandescent, a fluorescent, and a low-voltage halogen bulb (see pages 92–97) each give out a very different light which is dependent on the color temperature. The easily recognizable A lamp has a soft, yellow light which is warm and inviting at night but can seem dull in the daytime. The crisp whiteness of halogen light, on the other hand, is far better when used in dark areas during the day, as it is more compatible with daylight. At night, though, it can seem cool, but when dimmed will achieve the same warmth as the standard source.

A fluorescent source can be either cool or warm in color, depending on the fixture selected. When buying these lights, look for the particular code written on the packaging which gives the color temperature. Different light sources can be combined within a scheme if they are controlled separately.

The fixture's reflector (see page 98) also affects the color. For example, a gold reflector will give a warm quality to the light, whereas a silver reflector gives a slightly cooler light. Reflectors within some table lamp shades can also be gold or silver, and have a similar effect on the light.

*Control*

"Control" is the term lighting designers use for fine-tuning lighting to achieve maximum flexibility and ease of use: the more control a scheme has, the more flexible it is. It is highly recommended to separate the general lighting from both the feature lighting and task lighting. If only a single dimmer were used in each room for all lights, they would be dimmed together, and the relative brightness between the various light sources would remain the same. Control balances the lighting effects to create different atmospheres: at its simplest this is "on" or "off," bright or dim. However, a more complicated pre-set system (see page 90) can precisely balance all

the switchlines (see page 98) to exactly the right level and memorize them, so that, at the touch of a button, a different mood is instantly achieved. The advantage here is that you do not need to dim each switchline individually.

It is best to try to keep your light effects separate. If, for example, downlights and a lantern are providing your general light in a hall, they should be controlled individually and separately, because their light sources are different.

**1** Recessed, narrow-beam, low-voltage uplights highlight the flowers, whilst low-voltage lights skim out across each step creating a dramatic play of light and shadow.

**2** The low-voltage downlights, with frosted lenses, give a gentle, scalloped effect on the cabinets, and the narrow-beam downlights create a shaft of light on the stainless steel. There are also four downlights in the center providing a soft, general light on the floor.

1 The lighting from the gallery above spills into the kitchen. A narrow, downward focus of light on the table gives a sense of intimacy. Low-voltage down- and uplights give an unusual working light to the kitchen counter.

2 Layering of light creates different focuses in this large studio. Spotlights provide pools of light on objects and the library shelves, while local reading lights offer task lighting by the chairs. Care should be taken when positioning spotlights, so that their light is not thrown too far or creating unwanted glare.

## Light sources

These days, there are endless varieties of light sources. The main sources used in houses are incandescent, halogen, low-voltage, and compact fluorescent. Others, such as metal halide and sodium (see page 98), have a delayed start-up and are not easy to dim. For this reason they are used mainly in commercial situations rather than within the home, although they are sometimes useful in gardens to light up large trees and to provide the light source for fiber optics.

### Incandescent

This is the standard bulb in most of the table lamps we use and is available in a variety of shapes and sizes (see page 92). It has a tungsten filament, and light is produced by electrically heating the filament so that a mixture of light and heat is emitted. The resulting light is warm and inviting, which is effective in the evening, but can look unnatural and insipid during the day. For best results, this type of light source should be combined with others, so that a different balance is achieved between light levels for daytime and evening.

### Halogen

This bulb also contains a tungsten filament, but the filament is surrounded by halogen gas. The halogen combines with the tungsten to provide a far whiter and brighter light than the equivalent incandescent. It is often used for uplighting.

The halogen linear fixtures (200 to 300 watts), whether wall-mounted or free-standing, can be the perfect form of general light for a room with an ornate or sloped ceiling or unusual shape. The conventional halogen bulbs work very well as uplights, giving a white light and, with their high wattage, a correspondingly high level of illumination.

Incandescent bulbs can be used in bowl uplights to give a warmer, softer light than halogen. By contrast, where a high level of light is required, perhaps in a children's bedroom, family room, kitchen, or work area, the whiter light of the halogen source may be more appropriate.

### Low-voltage halogen

"Low voltage" means that a bulb fitting operates at 12 volts (v) rather than the usual 120v. The advantage of 12v is that the filament can be manufactured much smaller, which results in a more discreet light source that can still control the light efficiently. The spread of light is determined by the position of the filament within the reflector; if the filament is in the wrong place dark spots can appear in the light beam.

Low-voltage bulbs lend themselves especially well to feature lighting: they enable very precise control and provide an attractive white light because of their halogen gas. To reduce the voltage from 120v to 12v a transformer is required (see page 98). If a modern electronic transformer is used with downlights, it can usually fit through the aperture of the fixture and rest in the ceiling alongside the fixture. If maintenance is required, the transformer can be pulled out of the ceiling through the hole of the fixture itself.

### Fluorescent

Unlike an incandescent bulb, in which a filament is heated, this consists of a glass tube coated with a fluorescent phosphor powder and containing an inert low-pressure gas such as argon. When electricity is passed through the tube, the phosphorous layer is activated and emits light. Although four times more efficient than an incandescent, the light quality is much flatter and less focused, so is not normally used for feature lighting. It is often used as a task light under kitchen cabinets or as a general light source in a garage, but can also be used as an uplight under cabinets.

Smaller compact fluorescent sources can be used in downlights and, as long as they have special control equipment, such as a high-frequency dimmable ballast (see page 98), they can be dimmed. The start-up voltage required is provided by the ballast. When a tungsten filament is dimmed, less light is produced and the light becomes warmer in character; when a fluorescent is dimmed, the light source will also produce less light but the color temperature of the source will not change as the eye expects, and so sometimes produces a somewhat "gray," dull effect.

*Fiber optics*

The use of fiber optics is becoming more widespread. In essence, it uses an illuminator (see page 98). This remote light source focuses its light at one end of a bunch of individual glass fibers, and the light is transmitted down the fibers and is emitted at the end. This light is highly suitable for the display of sensitive items, because no heat or ultraviolet (UV) is emitted. It is also useful for providing light in places where access is problematic, as the illuminator can be placed in a more convenient location. The light source can be either metal halide or halogen, depending on the power required.

## Before you start

Before starting to plan the lighting for each room, look at the space to be lit. What are its best points? What atmosphere will be most appropriate? Identify the furniture plan within the room and where pictures and other important items will be positioned. Identify the color scheme and finishes so you know what will be reflective and what will not. Identify the key features in a room, i.e., the main accent points—are there niches, shelves, ornaments, or flowers on a table? What activities are to be performed in the room—reading, food preparation, etc.? Will special lighting be required? Does it need to be bright, or will a special task light be required? When you have addressed all of these issues, you are ready to begin designing your lighting scheme.

1. Incandescent is the standard bulb used in most decorative table lamps and wall lights, and provides a soft, warm light.

2. An incandescent striplight has the same soft light as an incandescent bulb, with a similar characteristic warmth, but the filament is long and surrounded by a glass tube. It resembles the fluorescent in shape, but its lamp life is far shorter.

3. Fiber optics provide a pattern of miniature stars on the ceiling. These are, in fact, created by a single light source, located remotely, which emits electricity down individual glass fibers in black sheaths, which emit light at their ends.

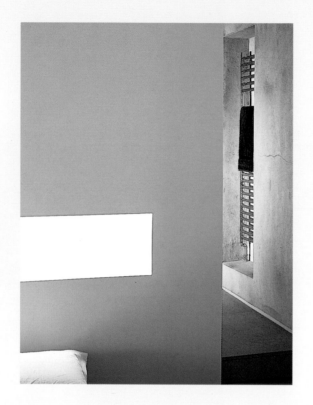

recipes and ideas

Designing lighting around the front door is vital, since it is the first introduction to your house. Lighting schemes can be designed to make an impact on the street or to be very discreet. At the entrance to your home, when the front door opens, hall lighting can be used to set the scene and create a wonderful impression by being both inviting and dramatic. Even in small spaces this is easy to achieve.

# entrances

Since entrance halls are often small, narrow spaces with little room for furniture, they require specific lighting solutions. The main objective when lighting a hall is therefore to create a bright, crisp effect, combining daylight and artificial light, to eliminate gloom. A common problem in narrow entrance halls is a shortage of natural light. If the hall is overlooked by a half-landing, a window at this position offers extra natural light and can act as a visual draw or focus to suggest space. This can also be achieved with artificial light at night.

1 The low-voltage downlights in this hall provide strong pools of light down the corridor and at the threshold of the room. This contrasts with the uplight over the curved doorway, which creates a general light in the living room.

2 This entrance is lit using a standard incandescent lamp in a lantern, which provides an all-over general light and lights a person at the door while creating an attractive visual focus.

This glass table is uplit from the floor using a 20w 12v narrow-beam lamp.

Narrow-beam directional lights at the end of the corridor create a focus on the picture.

Shallow 20w 12v downlights recessed into each shelf generously light each object.

Low-voltage downlights can be used to mimic daylight, but on their own they will make the ceiling seem lower and the space smaller, since the light falls solely on the floor. Uplighting emphasizes the ceiling and provides a feeling of spaciousness. The best solution is to layer the light by combining uplighting and downlighting or, perhaps, a decorative pendant with downlights. If you use a variety of light effects which can be switched on at will or controlled separately, the mood in the hall can be altered throughout the day. Wall-mounted fixtures do not often work in such a narrow space; uplights and downlights recessed into the walls, ceiling, or floor are therefore excellent alternatives.

A central pendant can be retained if in keeping with the style of the room but, if used alone, will produce a sharp, unattractive light. Supplement this with a pair of low-voltage downlights on either side to create a clean, daylight feel. Focus the downlights onto objects on the walls to provide a general wash.

Long corridors with no natural daylight require special attention. Various lighting elements can be used to create changing effects or highlight attractive features. For example, in a long, arched corridor cornice, recessed lighting could provide a soft, continuous wash of light on one side of the corridor, while recessed low-glare uplights could be used close to the opposite wall to emphasize the arch.

1 Downlights in a small space need not be centered; located close to one wall they create greater emphasis and a wall-wash effect.

An alternative way of making an entrance hall less gloomy is to create a focus in the middle distance. If a picture or object is lit on a half-landing, the eye will be drawn directly to this feature, distracting attention from the relative narrowness of the hall.

When lighting a very large hall, it is particularly important to create layers of lighting effects which you can alter during the day, since this may often be used as another living room or work space. You may wish to use a central decorative fixture; if so, another layer of light should be added. If you have a table below your central fixture, this layering could be achieved by adding a number of low-voltage downlights around the central pendant to focus on the table, where flowers or a selection of books could be placed.

The perimeter of the hall will require attention. Pictures could be highlighted, and a softness can be added to your lighting design by placing a lamp on a side table. Each of these effects, just as in any other room, would benefit from being controlled individually.

1  A spotlight, mounted on the wall above, lights the stair treads, and a downlight at the top of the stairs draws your eye upward. Two sculptured lamps provide soft, general light and serve as an interesting visual focus.

2  A small low-voltage downlight is recessed into each of the niches, which also produces a dramatic lighting effect on the objects. By lighting the niches enough light is also thrown onto the stairs.

3  This unusual collection of chandeliers provide an interesting sparkle effect; they can be dimmed to give a soft, candlelight glow. They contrast with the rustic brick chimney, which is covered with candles and lit with incandescent wall-washers, to offer a reflected light over the stairs.

## ways to light stairs

### Lighting the landing

Lighting a half-landing is a good way of also lighting stairs. Your eye is always drawn to the brightest point, here the half-landing, so you will almost be led up to the top of the stairs. The reflected light from the sources on the half-landing will also usually provide sufficient light for the stairs themselves.

### Floor accent lights

Floor accent lights, recessed into the wall, offer light over individual stair treads. A fixture with a wider wash could be located over every third or fourth tread. This technique is particularly useful when lighting basement stairs, where there are often limited locations for fixtures and the sloping ceiling of stairs above prevents the use of downlights.

28 recipes and ideas

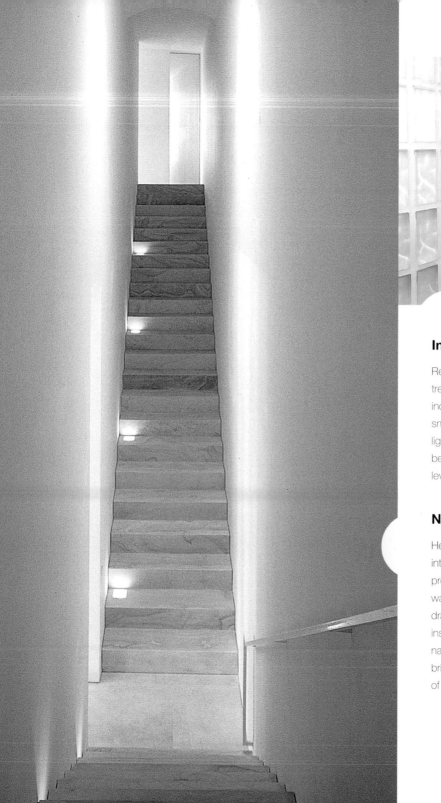

## Individual stair lights

Recessed lights, located in the stair tread above, will light the steps individually. This technique, using a small low-voltage light source, throws light across the step or floor, and can be used to accentuate a change of level within a room.

## Narrow stairs

Here the soft uplights are recessed into every fourth or fifth step to provide a wash over one of the side walls. This arrangement makes a dramatic statement that, in this instance, is used to emphasize the narrowness of the space. Again, a brighter light creates focus at the top of the stairs.

# ways to light a front door

## Downlights

For a contemporary style, recessed downlights throw light onto the front door and create a pool of light on the top step. Use a low-voltage baffled (see page 98) downlight with a wide-beam lamp, located as close to the front door as possible: this will achieve a high arc of light on the door itself while reducing any shadow on a visitor's face. Teaming a well-lit front door with a warm and welcoming entrance hall is the perfect way to use lighting to invite guests to enter the home and walk through to the living area.

## Up/downlights

Traditional wall lights could be replaced by something more original, such as a pair of up/downlights. These provide a strong architectural effect with their simultaneous lighting upward and downward. Used on each side of the door, particularly in a porch, these fixtures create a whole wash of bright light which makes a dramatic statement on the street and offers a vibrant welcome to guests. If you place a plant on either side of the front door, they will be put into dramatic silhouette by these lights.

## Traditional lantern

An effective welcome is to position
an incandescent hanging lantern
over the porch or to locate a pair of
decorative lantern-style wall lights
either side of the entrance. These
will provide a generous light on the
threshold. If guests need to walk
through a garden to the door, place
additional lanterns on an adjacent
wall, or, more dramatically, use stem-
mounted uplights (see page 98)
under plants and path lights (see
page 98) to light the way.

Whatever the style of your living or dining room, whether traditional or contemporary, the lighting should be an integral part of the design and should offer discreet solutions which are flexible enough for every activity. In a dining room the light should be bright, fresh, and appealing at lunchtime, and soft and subdued at night, allowing enough light on the table while avoiding harsh shadows on the diners' faces.

# living spaces

In rooms that are in regular use throughout the day and evening, the lighting must adapt to suit different moods or functions. Successful lighting depends on the general, feature, and task lighting working in harmony, in the same way that fabric colors and textures are chosen as part of the interior design. The solution you choose will depend on your style of decoration. By varying the levels of these individual effects, and by using different combinations, you can create both dramatic impact and the perfect light setting for every activity.

1 Rectangular slots in the ceiling are lit with an incandescent source, and the reflected light gives supplementary ambient lighting. The pendant in the double-height space provides enough light for the large area and serves as a visual focus.

2 The same space by day: natural light floods in and the slots in the ceiling remain in shadow, although the unlit pendant still acts as an interesting focus.

Although a single, central pendant may complement the style of the room, the light these fixtures produce is flat and dull. Used as a decorative feature, however, they do have their place as a focal point in the center of a room. To provide general lighting, they can be supplemented with other sources of light around the room, such as an arrangement of table lamps or wall lights.

Table lamps can be positioned anywhere within a room: to eliminate darkness around the edges; reduce areas of shadow in the center; or act as task lights for reading when located next to chairs and sofas. They thus introduce a second layer of light. It would be well worth installing floor outlets in the center of the room to give yourself more flexibility in choosing where to place lamps, and also to eliminate the problem of cords trailing from outlets at the edge of the room to your lamp. Although they are an easy option for a living room, too many lamps may give your home the appearance of a lighting store, and so it is advisable to combine these with other light sources.

In contemporary settings the general lighting is often achieved through methods other than pendants and table lamps. Downlighting, from fixtures installed in the ceiling or underneath cabinets, can effectively create a good overall light. If you choose this technique as part of your lighting scheme, standard-voltage fixtures could be used, but they are somewhat bulky and so it may be better to opt for the low-glare, low-voltage alternative. Another advantage of low-voltage downlights is their crisp, white light. On a gloomy day, their brilliant light makes it seem as if the sun is literally shining in, which means that they are particularly useful in rooms that receive little natural light.

Downlights are also very useful for adding light into the center of a room, an area that can sometimes be forgotten; they can be directed onto a decorative object to work as both general and feature lighting. Downlights placed directly over seating areas create effective reading lights, but can cast distorted shadows of light across those seated. If this task light is required, it would be useful to have the option of dimming the light to create a softer effect when entertaining.

A table lamp glows in the corner of the room, and candles work with flames from the fire to set the right mood.

A low-voltage uplight is concealed behind the chair to light the sculpture and balance the effect of the lamp.

Large lamps positioned beside the sofa provide both general and task lighting.

The picture light offers additional feature lighting and adds a highlight to the room.

## Framing pictures with light

When lighting a picture you need to consider where on the wall it is being hung, how to bring out the best color rendition, and the type of frame it has. For instance, is the frame relatively flat and unobtrusive or large and deep? If it is the latter, you must beware the frame casting ugly shadows over the picture. And if the picture has a heavy glaze or glass frame, the wrong kind of lighting will produce unwanted reflections. You need to consider where in the picture the detail is and whether an even wash of light or a specific focus would be more dramatic.

One of the most effective, but expensive, forms of picture lighting is to illuminate the whole picture surface evenly. This involves projecting a beam of light to the exact shape of the picture, which makes it appear as if it is internally illuminated. This is usually confined to the picture area, leaving the frame itself unlit. It is a startling technique which accentuates the impact of the picture. It can be achieved with a number of spotlights and a few recessed fixtures that use various lenses and shuttering devices (see page 98) to achieve the required result. Considerable care needs to be taken in their positioning to achieve the correct beam coverage and ensure that they are lined up exactly with the picture so that the shuttering devices can be used effectively to focus the beam of light.

# ways to light a picture

## Free-standing spotlight

The crisp, white light of low-voltage halogen helps to bring out a picture's true colors. If a picture with a glass cover is lit, unwanted reflections may occur. Here, a spotlight is used as an uplight, which means that reflections are not visible as they are reflected toward the ceiling. With a spotlight, you need to use the appropriate beam width for your picture: a narrow beam is suitable for small artworks.

## Frame-mounted light

With a picture light mounted on the frame, the picture should be effec-tively covered. An important consider-ation is the proximity of the light to the picture itself. If it is too close, the spread of light will cover only the top part of the picture. Additional light can be added, for example, from a table lamp located below. Avoid using wall-mounted picture lights, as they are more likely to light the wall instead.

## Directional downlight

A recessed, low-voltage directional downlight can be an effective picture light when baffled to prevent glare. You need to decide on the hanging height of the picture (usually eye level), to calculate the most effective beam width and the exact distance from the wall that the fitting will be recessed into the ceiling. For larger pictures two light sources may be necessary.

Uplighting is also a good solution for contemporary spaces, as most uplights are of a modern design. Low-level, drum-shaped uplights (see page 98), either standard- or low-voltage, can be hidden behind a piece of furniture to light the corners of a room or provide lighting in a bay window that appears dark at night. When positioned under plants, these uplights provide an interesting pattern of light on the walls and ceiling and contribute to both the general and feature lighting. A free-standing halogen uplight will provide a high intensity of light in rooms when required.

Wall-washing can be used to softly illuminate plain walls as an addition to the general lighting, or to highlight a favorite piece of art. Both effects can easily be achieved in your living or dining room by using an array of downlights positioned in the ceiling between 20–40 in. (50–100 cm.) away from a wall, depending on ceiling height, and 40 in. (100 cm.) apart. This works best if wide-beam bulbs are used, possibly with a frosted cover lens (see page 98). The brightness of this light may overshadow more subtle effects if it is not balanced by other areas of light on the opposite side of the room.

Having set the scene with the general and task lighting, you can introduce drama and contrast through feature lighting. Some of the choices you will have made for your overall lighting scheme may offer some feature lighting, but additional effects will add focus to chosen objects or areas of the room. Flowers on a coffee or dining table can, for instance, be illuminated with a narrow beam of light, which will bring out the best in the flowers and create a central focus in the room, making it appear more intimate.

1 A soft, low-voltage mini track, concealed by low benches, provides a gentle uplight. Maximum reflection is achieved with plain white walls.

2 In this case a light fixture becomes art itself and adds an extra dimension to the lighting within the room.

3 General light is provided by the wall lights, and low-voltage recessed lights are positioned to highlight the picture and the flowers on the coffee table as additional feature lighting. Lighting the center of rooms is important and is often forgotten.

Drama can also be created by highlighting architectural features of the room, whether a large open fireplace or an arched doorway. In a room with columns you can achieve stunning effects with lights recessed into the floor and positioned close to the column bases, as the light will graze up the side and produce a dramatic focus at the top.

The illumination of an alcove, shelves, or cabinet can be another form of focus and feature in a room. The simplest method of lighting shelves is to use an incandescent striplight, or tube, behind a baffle (see page 98) which conceals the source. There are, however, two disadvantages to this method: the bulky size of the fixture requires large shelf sizes to conceal the source, and the linear filament is delicate and frequently "blows." An alternative solution is to use candle bulbs, and although several individual bulbs are required, rather than a single linear source, they are cheaper than the incandescent strips and last much longer. Low-voltage shelf lighting systems, however, usually achieve the best results. They are smaller than the linear filament bulbs and therefore can be concealed within slimmer shelves. They normally consist of a small track system (see page 98), so that bulbs can be arranged either uniformly along the length of a shelf or in clusters to light specific objects. However, they do require a remote transformer (see page 98) and can get quite hot, so they should not be used near books. To light a bookshelf effectively, a simple standard-voltage rope-light (see page 97) can be used, since it offers a soft light, is fairly small, has a long lamp life, and does not get too hot.

Three-dimensional objects, like pieces of sculpture, offer the greatest scope for dramatic lighting. When lighting any object, the most important factors are the direction of light and the play between light and shadow, as distortions can result if the proportions and placing are not right. You must also consider the position from which the object will be viewed. Depending on the shape of the object, and the features within it that you wish to highlight, you can choose whether it should be uplit, downlit, or backlit. If you want to install your lighting before the piece to be lit has been chosen, cross lighting (see page 98) will be the safest option, as it allows you to throw light from both sides.

1 The pendant fixture is a strong visual focus: it softly accentuates the table, and the shade will help provide a soft, diffuse light on the diners' faces. The perimeter walls have strong feature lighting from recessed low-voltage sources.

2 Backlighting with a colored filter on the frosted-glass shelves provides a wash of atmospheric light to render the books in silhouette. The light becomes a theatrical backdrop here rather than functionally lighting the books.

## Combination of designs

Two lighting designs create subtly different effects. Downlighting through glass shelves creates interesting shadows, while the sidelighting in the central section of the cabinet gives a uniform warm glow. This combination lights the shelves but leaves the structure of the cabinet in shadow.

## Concealed light

Uplighting the cabinet itself creates more dramatic interest, highlighting the pilasters and creating pools of light over the architrave at the top. This is also a very successful way of providing indirect light in a room from a virtually concealed source.

creative lighting for display cabinets

## Downlighting

This miniature low-voltage downlight has a small baffle to reduce glare and is particularly good for bringing out the sparkle of glass objects. A 20w 12v, narrow-beam, dichroic MR11 bulb (see page 98) is powerful enough to punch light through the decanter and glass shelf to highlight the objects below. The decanter has been positioned to allow this light to pass through to the shelves below.

## Low-voltage light strip

A low-voltage light strip system is concealed by the side profiles of the cabinet. The fixture can use either 3w, 5w, or 8.5w 12v bulbs, at 2in. (5cm) intervals; if a larger gap were left, other areas of light and shade would be created. The effect here is a soft, even glow suitable for lighting most objects, whether ceramics, earthenware, or glass.

## Uplighting

Recessed low-voltage uplights set into the base of the unit employ 20w 12v, narrow-beam metal reflector bulbs, partially silvered to reduce the direct view of the light source. Light grazes the outside of the cabinet, while the objects themselves are lit by downlights flooding through the glass shelves above.

### Defining a route

Downlights emphasize the corridor route to the central dining area within this house. As the table remains unlit, it is not the natural focus within the room. For dining, an alternative lighting scheme is required.

### Filtered daylight

The venetian blinds allow a diffused light to wash over the dining table throughout the day, which is perfect for reading, working, relaxing, or lunchtime entertaining.

### The perfect setting

A narrow-beam spotlight provides a central focus for the table. Downlights emphasizing the corridor are dimmed to a candlelight level to create an air of intimacy.

successful
lighting for
dining rooms

decorative
lighting for a
chandelier

## Chandelier as a feature

A crystal chandelier can be a featured object as well as a light source. Often crystal light sources, when full on, can create unwanted glare. A simple step of installing a dimmer will reduce the output of the lamps and resulting glare, so that the chandelier draws more attention to itself as a decorative object. This can be further enhanced by installing four downlights into the ceiling above which are used to light the crystal itself.

## Focus above a table

In this dining room, two lights accentuate the shades, but the main focus is the chandelier, which provides the general light in the space. Used on its own, the light created would be flat and boring, but controlled separately from all other light sources the chandelier can be dimmed to a candlelight glow. The four low-voltage downlights shine through the chandelier to throw the flowers in the center of the table into dramatic relief.

Kitchens vary more in size than almost any other room, ranging from small, functional, and galley-style to spacious open-plan family rooms which may include sofas and a dining table. A flexible lighting scheme is required because a kitchen is not only often the center of family life, especially if there are children, but also used for entertaining friends as well as being the place for cooking and preparing food.

# kitchens

To reflect the wide range of functions that kitchens must fulfill, the lighting design should be flexible. It should adapt from a bright, general light for daytime—crucial in a dark kitchen as a supplement to daylight—to an intimate light in the evening. As with other rooms in your house, the first thing to consider is the general lighting. In the past, bare fluorescents were often chosen, as they provided a bright, diffuse light which created little shadow. However, besides being unattractive, their light can be too harsh for evenings.

1 Low-voltage downlights are located close to the cabinet fronts to accentuate the finish, light the surface, and supplement the under-cabinet lighting. By lighting the fronts of the cabinets, a spacious feel is created in this kitchen.

2 With no wall-mounted cabinets, this incandescent adjustable wall light can be twisted in any direction to provide a useful task light along the work surfaces.

Low-voltage downlights emphasize the front of the cabinets, increasing a sense of space.

Fluorescent tubes are concealed behind the frosted glass backsplash to light the top.

Downlights used over the range have sealed glass covers for easy cleaning.

The wide beam of slim cabinet lights, built into the niche, provides even light on the top shelf.

Track lighting has often been used in kitchens but is usually positioned wrongly in the center of the room, directing light at the kitchen worktops. If your kitchen were purely for show, this would be fine. But as soon as you work at a counter, your body is positioned between the light and the surface, which creates a shadow. The track therefore needs to be located much closer to the work surface, no more than 40 in. (1 m.) away from the cabinets. More than one track will usually be required to light a kitchen adequately, and the layout of the room may even call for a square arrangement of tracks. A small, galley kitchen is the only situation in which the central track method can be used successfully: it will automatically be close to the kitchen cabinets, and the light will shine over your head at the cabinet doors, the reflected light bouncing off to light all the kitchen worktops. An alternative to track is a cable system (see page 98). These cables appear almost invisible, and the individual bulbs can be adjusted along them to light as required.

In kitchens with low ceilings, spotlights and tracks may be unsightly and too much heat may be emitted from the lamps themselves. Fluorescent sources can be used, but you will achieve best effects by reflecting light off other surfaces. With a high ceiling, it may be possible to conceal a fluorescent lamp on top of the cabinets to create a successful general light reflecting off the ceiling. However, using fluorescents directly as downlights can instill the atmosphere of an industrial kitchen rather than a domestic one. Their other main disadvantage is their poor quality of light, compared to halogen. Fluorescent light has a flat quality which gives an excellent working light, but does not bring out the best in surface finishes.

The choice of the color of fluorescent bulbs is also important: a cool, white fluorescent light can appear too harsh, while the warmer lights can appear slightly "dirty." Fluorescent is difficult to dim, and so at night can be too harsh. If you are certain you wish to use fluorescents and would like to be able to dim the lights, you will need to power them with high-frequency, dimmable ballasts (see page 98) which can be expensive.

Halogen fixtures can be used as uplights to provide the general lighting in a kitchen. They are simpler to dim than fluorescent fixtures, but far less energy-efficient. Whichever you use, you will almost certainly require some form of task highlights as well, possibly over a central island or under the kitchen cabinets.

The most effective and attractive kitchen technique is to use recessed downlights arranged regularly with wide-beam bulbs. Besides appearing far neater than a surface-mounted track and spotlights, they are also less susceptible to the gathering of grease, dust, and dirt of a surface spotlight. The usual mistake, however, is to position the downlights in the center of the room so that they focus on the floor rather than

the perimeters of the room. Without good task lighting, the perimeter work surfaces will be poorly lit and, because the units themselves are not lit, the walls will appear dark.

With the design of modern kitchen units using natural materials or painted decorative finishes, it is best to direct the light at the front of the cabinets and units to give reflected light to your work surfaces. This has the benefit not only of directing the light where it is required, but also of making the kitchen appear brighter, as all the vertical surfaces are lit. The neatest downlights are low-voltage. They have the added benefit of giving a daylight quality to your lighting, which can be very important in a basement kitchen, yet when dimmed will provide a much softer light.

Task lighting in a kitchen is as important as the general lighting. If possible it should be controlled separately from the general lighting. Usually there are two main types of task lighting in a kitchen: under-cabinet lighting and the lighting of a central island. Under-cabinet lighting normally falls into three categories, fluorescent, incandescent tubes, and low-voltage lighting.

Fluorescent is cool running and has a long lamp life but generally does not give the soft, intimate light that you may require for a dimmed supper setting. Moreover, if your worktops are very reflective, made of polished granite or a similar material, fluorescent light can produce rather unsightly reflections.

1. The lighting on the ceiling and cornice is the diffuse "borrowed" light from the room beyond the glass screen. An incandescent spotlight is clipped to the central stem of the island, so that the light beam can easily be adjusted to focus where required.

2. A number of low-voltage lamps on flexible arms can be twisted in any direction, providing an unusual, decorative, and functional light to the central work area. The background lighting is from incandescent lamps in industrial-style aluminum reflectors.

3. Recessed downlights provide an arc of light over the walls in this kitchen, and a ceiling pendant with a wide reflector lights the island. Another downlight highlights the stainless steel extractor fan over the range.

1. Halogen uplights in this high-ceilinged room provide the general light and combine effectively with low-voltage under-cabinet lights, which create interesting reflections on the stainless steel.

2. A single low-voltage downlight creates emphasis on the oven hood. The granite on either side is also lit by low-voltage downlights, but these are positioned very close to the wall.

3. The feature low-voltage up/downlights provide the fill light, while task light is created by discreet, built-in, low-voltage sources over the oven and sink unit.

4. Fluorescent under-counter light gives a flat, even working light, but is successful only if the worktop is non-reflective.

Incandescent tubes provide a soft glow but have several disadvantages. Because their linear tungsten filaments are fragile, the bulbs tend to blow quite often, especially with frequent banging of cabinet doors. They also get quite hot, which may be a problem if food is stored in the cabinets above.

A low-voltage under-cabinet fixture is one of the best solutions. Not only is the low-voltage light far brighter and crisper than its competitors when on full, it provides, when dimmed, a candle-like quality. Because they are only ¾ in. (2 cm.) deep, low-voltage bulbs can be recessed into the base of cabinets or surface-mounted behind a small cornice board. Their main disadvantages are that they are more expensive to install and their lamp life is shorter than that of a fluorescent source; however, their light is infinitely more enhancing to the work surface finish. And dimming will certainly prolong their lamp life.

The central island of a kitchen often needs additional task lighting. This can be achieved with an arrangement of downlights above it, controlled independently from all over lights in the room. Alternatively, if a hanging device for pots and pans is positioned over the island, downlights can be incorporated into this. It is best for the lighting to be located within the hanging device itself to avoid the possibility of shadows. Pendants will provide an unusual decorative, effect, as well as a soft focus of light over the island.

feature lighting for kitchen back-splashes

## Innovative task lighting

Innovative methods of task lighting include designing a frosted glass back to the cabinets, and back-lighting them with either fluorescent or low-voltage sources. Fluorescent light will give a more even effect, while low-voltage will provide an attractive scalloped design behind the glass, as shown here. The table in the foreground has low-voltage downlights cross-lighting the surface as a useful task light.

## Front light

The back-lighting alone puts the pans into silhouette, and a soft, low-voltage front light emphasizes the stainless steel finishes. Being controlled separately, the front light can be used independently of the back light.

## Back light

The low-voltage back light is successful, as the wall behind the glass is painted white to maximize reflection. This provides an almost even light, putting all the contents of the shelves into dramatic silhouette.

In bedrooms, effective task lighting is necessary for nighttime reading and around dressing tables, and the general light needs to adapt to every requirement of the changing seasons: on a dark winter morning, low-voltage bright lights will provide early risers with a feeling of get-up-and-go. The lighting should also be strong enough to distinguish between the blue and black of your clothes in the closet.

# bedrooms

When designing a lighting scheme for a bedroom, it is essential that each of the chosen effects be easily adjustable, according to the mood you wish to create or the brightness of light required. As this is the last room to be seen at night and the first room to be seen in the morning, you need lighting that will bring a calming atmosphere at night, with task lighting for reading and around a dressing table, and a refreshing wash of light when you awake.

1 A concealed linear light source built into the wall directly behind the head of the bed not only acts as an architectural delineation but also provides effective light for reading.

2 These dramatic uplights provide general light in the room and some light for the bed. If you want a reading light, however, it would be best to combine these with a more localized source.

For a general wash of light, particularly if your bedroom has a fairly low ceiling, downlights can be effective if they reflect their light to the walls and floor and are used in conjunction with table lamps. If bright light is unnecessary, table lamps strategically positioned around the bedroom can often be enough. This would normally consist of four fixtures: two on either side of your bed and one or two on a chest of drawers or desk. In addition, you could place a floor lamp behind a chair. If your ceiling is high, you could consider uplighting, using wall-mounted fixtures. Halogen floodlights can be located on top of cabinets or wardrobes to create an almost invisible source of bright uplight, reflecting off the ceiling.

With feature lighting, unusual effects can be achieved within a bedroom. Some can be soft and subtle, and some dramatic at night. You can achieve a beautifully soft glow by placing a linear light under the bed (see pages 96–7), so that the bed itself, in the center of the space, will seem almost to float. A similar effect can be achieved by lighting under the bottom of shelves, particularly if the shelves are in a recess.

Other dramatic effects include a "star-lit" ceiling made by small fiber-optic heads only slightly piercing the ceiling and giving the impression of sleeping out under the stars. When these are turned off, the ceiling will appear no different from any other, but at nighttime, with the lights on, it gives the effect of numerous small stars.

More common feature lighting effects also work well in bedrooms, and may be appropriate to the style of room and decoration. You could light a prominently placed picture, use uplighting under a bay window to highlight your draperies, or choose favorite ornaments to become your lighting focus.

When the general and feature lighting is decided, the task lighting must be considered. For a dressing table, you will achieve the most flattering facial light by placing lights on either side of the mirror. An ideal solution is to use two separate lamps. It is important that the shades not be colored, so that a natural light will be thrown onto your face.

An efficient reading light is essential in a bedroom. The ultimate in bedroom task lights, used in conjunction with bedside table lamps, is the fiber-optic flexi-light. This is fixed to the wall at shoulder height and provides a completely flexibly positioned bright reading light. The fiber-optic illuminator (see page 98) would be located under the bed.

A more traditional source of reading light is a table lamp placed on each side of the bed, but these must be correctly positioned if eyestrain and awkward posture are to be avoided. If lamps are located on a bedside table, the light is often in the wrong place, almost forcing you to lean out of bed to read. You need to achieve the right balance between the size of the lamp and the height of the table. If the table is too high, the glare of the lamp will shine into your eyes and the

spread of light will be too wide. The ideal height for the base of the shade is at shoulder level when you are sitting up in bed.

An alternative to table lamps is an adjustable wall light on an extendable bracket (see page 98), with arm extensions or a swing arm. As this is wall mounted, you can control the precise height and position of the lamp, but you will need to know the height and size of the bed before installation.

If you want to create a pool of light purely for reading, and your ceiling is not too high, an effective solution is to use a low-voltage spotlight with a narrow-beam lamp on a dimmer. Again, before installation you will need to be certain of your reading position in bed so that the spotlight is placed at the correct point on the ceiling.

Task lighting is also necessary for a wardrobe or closet. Low-voltage downlights, with frosted lenses, will provide a soft wash over the front of the doors. A concealed linear strip could be used above the wardrobe, or door-operated lighting (see page 98) could be installed for automatic light.

In most bedrooms you will need at least two switch-lines (see page 98) to control your different light sources: one for bedside lamps and one for other lamps. If you are using either uplights or downlights, these will need a third switch. With a double bed, it may be easier to control each bedside light individually, which will add another switchline. Two-way switching to the bedside works well, as all lights can be turned on and off from the bed. A dimmer, either by the door or at the side of the bed, will give easy control.

1 These closets are lit by a concealed linear, low-voltage incandescent source in a trough mounted at the junction between wall and ceiling, to provide a soft, continuous wash of light. The light in this room is for decorative purposes but also helps with task requirements when clothes need to be found.

2 In a room that has a rush of natural light, keeping all walls and surfaces plain white will allow for ultimate reflection. Here the closets are lit from behind, casting the objects within into silhouette and creating an unusual feature.

reading
lights in the
bedroom

## Downlights

Low-voltage downlights with a well-recessed light source can be controlled individually to provide effective reading lights for both sides of the bed. They also offer a wash of general light to the rest of the room. They need to be controlled individually on each side of the bed.

## Fiber optics

The ultimate fiber-optic bedside light, built into this headboard provides a dedicated reading light and, as its beam is so precise, will literally light only your book. The table lamp adds a softness to the atmosphere of the room when ambient light is required.

## Wall lights

These two wall-mounted bedside lights create good reading light on either side of the bed. They are at the correct height to light over the shoulder when reading in bed and are low enough to ensure that the light source is still concealed.

Until fairly recently bathrooms were designed as purely functional rooms, but in contemporary homes they have taken on a new role as a sanctuary of relaxation. There is often little natural light in a bathroom, so your lighting design needs to complement the style of the room and be flexible enough to change from bright and invigorating in the morning to a softer, more subdued ambience for evening baths.

# bathrooms

The location of your light fixtures is crucial within a bathroom, partly because of the potential safety hazards, but also because many of the surface finishes are very reflective. Crisp low-voltage halogen light reflects particularly well off these surfaces, and its success has given rise to a range of new lighting techniques. Instead of a regular grid of downlights in the ceiling, you could consider locating the lights directly over your basin and bathtub; when they are filled, a wonderful pattern of rippling water will be reflected across the ceiling.

1 Recessed low-voltage fixtures uplight the thick glass vanity top and emphasize the textured glass surface. A purely decorative effect, this needs to be combined with a practical downlight for lighting the face.

2 A low-voltage downlight catches the glass screen at the end of the bathtub and highlights the chrome tap. Other downlights, close to the glass walls at the back, provide an arc of light to wash the walls and floor.

If you do not want downlights directly overhead and if the bathtub is against a wall, you could position a series of small low-voltage downlights in the ceiling, approximately 4 in. (10 cm.) from the wall. This will create a beautiful scalloped pattern, suggesting water streaming down the tiles, and is also a good way of lighting a shower unit.

Besides the practicalities of your bathroom lighting you will need to consider your feature elements. For example, if there is a niche for ornaments, a small downlight could be installed within this to highlight objects on a shelf or to light all the way through if the shelving unit is glass.

By lighting underneath the bathtub, it can appear almost to float. A soft ropelight (see page 97) concealed beneath the tub surround will give a continuous soft, even glow and could almost be used as a nightlight because of its low brightness. Alternatively, a row of small spotlights could be recessed around the base of the tub to skim out across the floor in strong shafts of light. This is a dramatic effect which can look magnificent in a modern bathroom. To achieve this successfully, it is essential to use low-voltage baffled lights of no more than 12w 12v and to ensure that they are fully sealed behind glass; otherwise the heat of the

1  Lights located close to the back wall create a scalloped pattern down the wall. For best results these should be no more than 4 in. (10 cm.) from the wall to ensure that the arc of light is high on the wall.

2  A continuous fluorescent strip of light is used both above and below the mirror. The light below emphasizes the marble surfaces, and the light above creates a general, daytime wash, which is also an excellent shadow-free light for the face.

3  Low-voltage downlights are located close to the rear wall of the shower, while two fixtures are directed down onto the bathtub, making it a sculptural focal point within the space.

light could scald the feet of anyone standing near the tub.

If your washbasin is made of glass, recessing an uplight below it creates a stunning effect, making the basin appear to be lit internally. This will need to be balanced by a downlight, or your face will appear rather ghostly. The uplight should be fully sealed and the beam of the lamp wide enough to ensure maximum coverage of the glass bowl itself. For applying makeup, the ideal lighting is the kind traditionally used in the theater—strips of small individual lamps around the mirror. These are available in frosted or clear glass, on a wood, metal, and mirror strips.

If you control each area of your lighting separately, it will be more adaptable to your changing needs. Dimming will make your lighting work at all times of the day, from "full on" in the morning to a soft, subdued effect at night.

In bathrooms, safety is of crucial importance. Make sure that any fixture you install is UL-listed as suitable for "damp" locations. If children use the bathroom, it is a good idea to have the main light controlled by a pull cord, rather than a switch. Before planning any work in the bathroom it is essential to consult a professional and check the local safety regulations.

## Incandescent wash

Unless a shower is properly lit, there is a danger that it will become an unattractive dark hole in your bathroom. Fortunately, there is a wide range of fully water-resistant fixtures now available which cater to all tastes and demands.

Here, the gray concrete shower is lit by a simple incandescent wall-mounted fixture. Additional natural light is filtered into the space through a textured glass wall on one side, creating reflections on the opposite side. The warmth of the incandescent bulb, in its perfect circular fixture, provides a very warm, diffuse light on the shower base and contrasts with the diffused light through the glass wall.

## Scalloped downlights

The scalloping effect of low-voltage downlights works particularly well in showers, as it helps to draw your eye toward the rear wall and gives the impression of extra space. Alternatively, lights recessed into the side wall of a shower, using a directional spreader lens (see page 98), will deflect the light to the rear walls. You should aim to direct the lights down onto the back wall; their visual appearance on the side wall will suggest a number of portholes. The spreader lenses are usually part of the fixture itself, or in some cases can be ordered as a special attachment.

Here, the two low-voltage downlights reflect off the blue tiled wall of the shower to provide a strong focal point within the bathroom.

*Note:* As safety is of such great importance within a bathroom, it is advisable to use low-voltage light sources since they reduce almost all of the hazards of standard-voltage fixtures. A glass cover over the lamp fixture is, however, recommended in case they are splashed: halogen bulbs can, on very rare occasions, shatter, and a glass screen will protect you from any accidents.

ways
to light
showers

## Recessed mirror light

One of the priorities in a bathroom is the lighting around the mirror. If this is done badly, your face will either be completely in shadow or have unsightly dark shadows cast across it. A single low-voltage downlight positioned over the basin looks magnificent but casts shadows on the features of anyone looking into the mirror. A single downlight source can, however, be supplemented with other lighting effects. For example, if the downlight is directed slightly toward the mirror, as here, the reflected light will be more diffuse and reduce the shadowing.

If the basin is a light color, then the downlight will be reflected back up and increase the general effect. The ideal solution is to have side lighting from a diffuse source on either side of the mirror, or, even better, as a continuous strip around the mirror, as shown here. This achieves virtually no shadowing and gives the most even modeling of the face.

ways to light a mirror

## Concealed lighting

General lighting here is created by the backlighting of the glass in the niche, combined with the downlights washing the front of the frosted glass behind the mirror. The specific highlight to the face is from an incandescent light concealed within the mirror.

## Striplights

In this bathroom, two incandescent striplights provide a soft, even light to the face, while the low-voltage downlights, centered on each basin, enhance the surface color and texture. If the downlight alone is used, shadow will be created on the face.

More and more people are now working from home, either from a desk area in the corner of a living room or bedroom or in a separate office. Working for long periods of time, particularly on the computer, requires very specific solutions in order that the right environment for focused work is created and headaches and eyestrain are avoided. If the work space is part of another room, flexibility is essential.

# work spaces

Unlike most other rooms, the most important requirement when lighting a work area is an effective task light. A successful balance must be achieved between this and the general lighting to avoid eyestrain, which can result from the contrast between a well-lit surface and dark surrounding walls, or if too much light is reflecting onto a screen. Feature lighting is not essential, but will be effective in creating more atmosphere in a room where you have to spend time, and could be used to highlight a bookshelf or a picture.

1 An adjustable table lamp allows great control over the direction of light over the desk. Three low-voltage downlights, recessed into the ceiling, also provide general light directly onto the working area, separating it from other parts of the room.

2 The same space by day, with natural light filtered through the venetian blinds allowing enough light onto the desk.

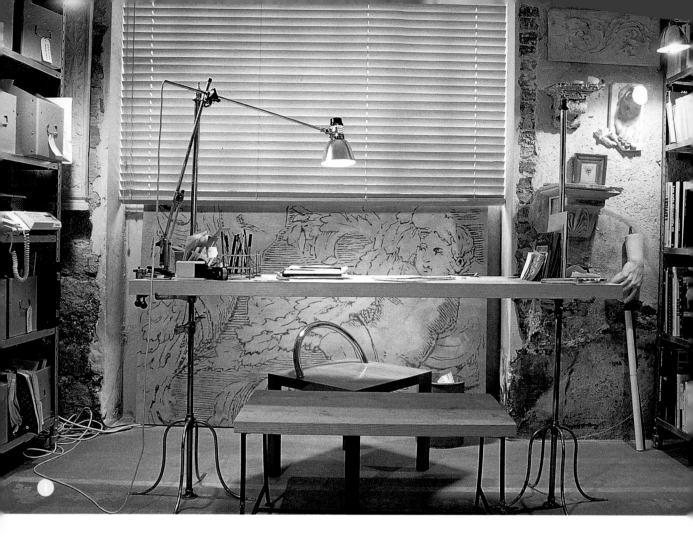

Task lighting could be provided by a desk lamp or, if there are shelves above the desk, by lighting fixed to, or underneath, the shelves. Desk lamps and those fixed to shelves offer a degree of adaptability as the direction of their lamp beam can be adjusted. A movable light will work very well if a computer is to be used, since the amount of light and any reflection on the screen can be fully controlled. Whichever solution is chosen, the task light should, if possible, be on a separate switch from all other sources in the room so that it creates focus on the work area only.

The general lighting is probably most efficiently provided by a free-standing uplight, which will create a soft,
diffuse light without casting problematic reflections on the computer screen; these reflections may occur when using downlights in your overall scheme.

If the room has shelves, other sources can be employed. If there is a gap of at least 24 in. (60 cm.) between the top shelf and the ceiling, an uplight can be incorporated above the shelf. If the gap is smaller than 24 in. (60 cm.), a continuous source, such as overlapping fluorescent tubes or xenon striplights, will be more successful than a halogen uplight, which would create more of a "hotspot" of intense light on the ceiling rather than provide a general wash over the room.

If you have a whole wall of shelving or a library, low-voltage track lighting will give enough light for you to see every book on each shelf. Alternatively, traditional library lights can be employed. Sometimes also called French library lights, these are usually wall-mounted on brackets, and can have one-, two- or three-arm connections depending on the extension and versatility required. Originating from the idea of a candle on a vertical pole, with an arm-extension so that the lamp could be shifted upward or sideways, they offer a focused light that can be moved across the shelves. The electrical versions provide the same versatility for both contemporary and traditional interiors.

1 A home office, with two adjustable table-mounted lamps for the desk area to provide task light when necessary. Shelf-mounted lights create general light in the room but can also be adjusted to become task lights over the shelves.

2 A table lamp, with a wide reflector and pale shade, gives a wash of light over the desk for letter writing. General light is provided by sources in other areas of the room.

3 A number of light sources create a good general light in this office, with a combination of table lamps, ceiling pendant, and a free-standing lamp for extra light when required.

Your garden can be such a pleasure during the day, but is it forgotten at night? Even if it is small, a garden could become an extra room in your house and provide an added dimension to the character of your home. If your garden has a well-designed lighting scheme, your eye will be drawn outside to all the features you have lit, and the feeling of space will expand to include the area surrounding your home.

# gardens

A garden can appear magical at night if you simply light a few carefully chosen features. Even a lantern in a small summerhouse can be enough to provide a glow or focus. A little light goes a long way at night; it is therefore important to decide what features to light and to what intensity.

Garden lighting can be problematic. One example of this is the "security light" approach, in which a halogen light located above a door or window gives an overall flood of light, but will not create any atmospheric or feature lighting.

1 Candles define the edges of the veranda, but table and floor lamps are brought out with the furniture to create a room outside. It is always worth positioning outlets to allow for temporary lighting on verandas used as outdoor seating areas.

2 An urn in the distance is a striking focus when lit; here, the light stone contrasts brightly against the dark green hedging. A small concealed halogen flood is located approximately 40 in. (1 m.) in front of the urn and lights the structure evenly.

This use of a single halogen light source is tolerable when the garden is viewed from inside, though it does give a rather flat light. However, when you sit in the garden it is intolerable to look at, creating glare and an unwelcoming harshness.

As with interiors, exterior lighting can be broken down into various functions, such as lighting pathways, defining an entrance, lighting a vista or a feature, lighting a terrace for dining, and security.

The first priority for landscape lighting is to identify the main features you wish to light; this can vary from a landscape item, such as a tree or shrub, to an architectural feature such as a pergola, statue, folly, or arch. Your method of lighting will vary depending on the feature. As with interior lighting, the key to successful lighting is to conceal the light source, so unless you wish to make a feature of the lamp itself, you see only the lighting effect. For example, a folly, bridge, or summerhouse at the end of a garden could be lit with a small floodlight, so long as this feature is viewed from only one direction. If the garden is used at night, this approach could create unwanted glare from some approaches, so more discreet lighting would be required.

Garden light fixtures generally tend to be black, but the neatest ones to look for are those finished in dark green, as they blend in with the foliage more effectively. Copper fixtures can be similarly effective, as they will patinate to a natural green color with age. Bronze fixtures are also suitable, particularly if they are mounted in a tree, as they blend in with the color of the trunk.

1  The wall lights are simple, yet
their effect is dramatic. A single
light source has been cleverly
fitted with a special directional
lens to throw a narrow shaft of
light upward, and a wide beam
downward, over this outdoor
patio area.

2  The background lighting on the
terrace is created by miniature
green, stem-mounted, low-voltage uplights which light the trunk
of each copper beech tree and
catch the foliage around. The
spill of light is reflected off the
perimeter white walls. Two more
spotlights at the planting edge,
concealed by two of the pots,
are directed toward the large
corner pot, to create front lighting. Candles have also been
chosen to help set the mood.

3  The door is framed by the large,
pyramidal structures with incandescent light sources within. The
light sources shine through the
metal frames of the fixtures to
cast a wonderful pattern across
the back wall.

## Topiary

Putting trees into silhouette is an effective way of lighting them, so in some cases they may be a specific feature, but in others, their shape and form are defined by lighting the walls or buildings behind.

I rarely use colored lamps in gardens, as I feel that plants have enough natural color. It is best to highlight plants using a white light to bring out their true color during the changing seasons.

Here an up/downlight has been used, which creates a feature of the light source as well as a dramatic silhouette of the tree. The base of the tree is highlighted with four small, green, low-voltage stem-mounted lights, with a transformer located under the base of the wooden pot.

## Low-level plants and stone

Statues are often best lit using a small staked spotlight concealed by foliage. If you are lighting a statue in the center of a lawn, a fully recessed adjustable uplight would be the most discreet solution, which also prevents problems when mowing the lawn. Low-level shrubbery is a useful way to conceal a light fixture, but can still allow the light to filter through, so long as the foliage around the light fixture is trimmed regularly. Here, candles light each step, and two uplights on stems are used, one uplighting the tree and the other highlighting the well.

ways
to light
a garden
feature

## Lighting a trellis and path

Lighting a trellis can create a wonderful effect, not only by lighting the foliage that grows up it but by accentuating the trellis design. A diamond-shaped trellis, for example, will create a strong diagonal pattern; by highlighting the foliage you can slightly soften this strong architectural effect.

Paths, steps, and terraces need to be illuminated to provide easy access from your house to the garden or from one part of the garden to another. One way of lighting a path is to rely on reflected light provided by lighting features such as planting or trees. This is normally adequate to light a level path, but special attention needs to be made to light any changes in level. A small spotlight could be located in a tree, lighting downward using the "moonlighting" method (see page 98), or a localized source can be built into the step or be provided by a small copper "mushroom-" style fixture or various types of bollard light (see page 98). These should be green, if possible, to blend in with the foliage.

Here the path and trellis have been lit using a garland of Christmas tree lights wound around both the low-level box hedging and the trellis arch.

## Lighting a pergola and trees

A pergola presents another interesting structure for lighting. Normally, it covers a walkway leading to a feature which could be lit to provide a strong visual focus. A pergola could be uplit, highlighting the framework as well as lighting the canopy. A small spot could be concealed at high level to light down through, or across the foliage at canopy level. Up/downlights could also be mounted halfway up the pergola to create more definition.

Just as for interior lighting, a fixture with a baffled light source is most appropriate, so that the light source can be concealed and the effect of the light maximized.

Concealing lights up the tree trunk can be a very effective way of lighting a tree with a large canopy. Halogen or metal halide sources can be effective, but it is recommended that some form of baffle or glare shield be used. Invariably the fixture will need to be tilted out to light the canopy fully, and "barn door" attachments (see page 98) can be used to conceal the light source. With this method there is less likelihood of the effect becoming overgrown and lost.

Here, small, green 50w 12v reflectors throw light across the path, while three 50w 12v stem-mounted spotlights emphasize the ladder and tree beyond the table.

practicalities

## Planning your lighting

Before embarking on a new electrical installation it is worth having your existing wiring and breaker panel (or fuse panel) checked. Very old houses will probably not have the power capacity required and may need to be rewired. Fuses that continually blow are a good indication of an over-loaded system. Modern lighting techniques require more outlets compared to the old approach, which relied mainly on a single hanging fixture plus a few lamps. This may involve wiring a separate circuit back to the main entrance panel to take the additional load. For any installation it is always best to use a qualified electrician. Electricity is potentially dangerous, and for this reason installing wiring and light fixtures is subject to strict regulations which need to be adhered to. These vary from country to country, but a qualified electrician will be well aware of the requirements.

## Checklist of things to do before planning your lighting

1 Start by making a sketch plan of the room to scale, putting all the furniture and key pictures or ornaments in position. Note all the existing outlets, as some of these could be re-used.

2 Think about the activities that will be taking place in the room and how much general light and task light they will require.

3 Decide which light sources and techniques to use for the general light and where they should be placed for best effect. Note that a pale interior will reflect more light than a dark interior.

4 Make a note on the plan of the position of any feature light sources and what these sources will be. If using downlights to light an object on a wall, remember that the height of the ceiling will determine how far from the wall the fixture should be positioned.

5 One you have established the various lighting types, it is useful to consider how they will be controlled. A good system will separately switch or dim each lighting element in a room.

## Checklist of things to consider when undertaking a new installation

1 Make sure that you have enough outlets in the room. Remember that trailing cords may cause accidents, so it is a good idea to install floor outlets in the center of the room if lamps are required around a sofa or table away from the walls.

2 If you want to install recessed downlights, check that there is a ceiling cavity and how deep this is. It is important to know what the ceiling is made of; the mounting brackets of the fixture will need to be checked to ensure that they are compatible with the ceiling type.

3 Ascertain whether the ceiling contains insulation. If it does, you must buy a fixture marked "IC" (insulation-compatible), which includes a buffer to prevent contact between the lamp and the insulation; otherwise, you can use a "non-IC" fixture.

4 Recessed uplights in floors can get very hot unless fiber optics are used (which are very expensive). The position of these uplights needs to be considered carefully, as they can cause burn. Their use should be limited to feature lighting, which can be switched off if children are around.

5 Any lighting fixture you buy should bear the UL stamp, which means that it has been approved by the Underwriters' Laboratories, Inc. A mark from this independent testing laboratory ensures that the item meets the minimum safety requirements. It also specifies whether a light fixture is suitable for different locations, such as "damp" (suitable for bathrooms) and "wet" (outdoors).

6 The positioning of all light fixtures is crucial: they should not be located too close to flammable materials or to the ceiling, as scorch marks may result. The installation instructions should state a minimum safe distance; if not, consult the manufacturer.

7 Check the position of switches. If you are changing the way a door swings, remember to change the switch position.

8 For exterior installations, ensure that all cables are mounted well away from areas that may need digging or regular mowing. If cables are located in the center of a garden, they should be a minimum of 18 in. (45 cm.) underground.

1 At high level a narrow-beam, low-voltage spotlight highlights the table in this courtyard. A visual focus is created by the dramatic up/downlight on the back wall of the interior.

planning your lighting | 89

## Control

Once you have established the various types of lighting, it is useful to consider how they will be controlled. A good system will separately switch or dim each lighting element in a room. The first stage is to switch each effect or element separately—that is, the general lighting separately from the accent lighting and task lighting. Almost all rooms benefit from this degree of adaptability over the balance of light and the mood. Another advantage of using a dimmer is that they extend the life of filament bulbs, including incandescent, conventional halogen, and low-voltage light sources.

A dimmer has a maximum load which cannot be exceeded, and so the correct size must be used for the amount of wattage you wish to dim. It should also be noted that a dimmer has a minimum load rating; if this is not reached the light source may flicker. The most usual dimmer is the rotary type, but there are also sliders and touch-plate controls. As the dimmer is working it may emit a low hum. If you are sensitive to this, it is worthwhile considering locating the dimmer outside the room or using a pre-set dimmer system. If the hum is very audible, there may be a fault with the dimmer module itself. This can easily be checked, and changed if necessary, by an electrician.

With standard dimming the lights can be dimmed only from one position, so with two-way switching you will be able to switch the lights on or off only at the level to which they were previously set. It is therefore important to consider the best location for the switch. Pre-set lighting is commonly used in hotels, but is becoming increasingly popular in the home, as it removes the need for a bank of four to six dimmer knobs and large plates in a room. The plate usually has four scenes (buttons) offering pre-set "moods" and an off button. For each "mood" the lighting has effectively been pre-set to suit that particular time of day. It is similar to having to adjust the levels of each light source manually and then memorizing that exact dimmed level. Most pre-sets also offer a raise-and-lower facility so that the scene can be further dimmed if required without losing the original setting.

*In a living room, typical settings would be:*

Scene 1   Bright—daytime

Scene 2   Softer—early evening

Scene 3   More dramatic—after dinner

Scene 4   TV mode

*In a kitchen / breakfast room:*

Scene 1   Bright

Scene 2   More subdued, but focused over counters

Scene 3   Dinner setting for evening entertaining

Scene 4   Low-level for just popping into the kitchen quickly

*Photocell control*

A photocell instructs the lights to come on when it is dark and is recommended for all garden installations, as it prevents the lights from being accidentally switched on during the day. Once switched on they will remain off during the day, only coming on when it is dark. They can easily be switched on or off at any time when required.

*Motion sensor*

A motion sensor consists of an infrared detector that switches a light on when it detects movement, and is best linked to a photocell to prevent daytime operation. It is particularly useful when used to control entrance and security lights, switching the lights on for a set length of time (say 2–3 minutes) and then switching off again. It is recommended that these sensors have an override on/off switch, so that if used in conjunction with security lights, these can be switched off when necessary.

*Timer*

A timer can set your lights to come on and go off again at specific times of the day, and are often used in conjunction with photocells. They can also be linked into a pre-set control system, so that different scenes can be switched on and off when the house is empty, to make it appear as if someone is there.

# Fixtures

## Baffles

A baffle is a device, usually a metal or wood shield, attached to a light fitting to conceal the bulb from direct view, which helps to prevent glare. When designing a baffle to conceal a light source, you must consider all viewing angles, particularly when locating fittings at the side of a cabinet, in shelves or under cabinets, etc. It is important to include a return baffle when a light source is used in shelves, to conceal the light source completely on both sides as well as from the front, so that you are only aware of the effect of light on the shelves rather than being distracted by the light itself.

## Lampshades

The design of lampshade you choose will have an impact on your overall lighting scheme, as different shades have different effects. A light-colored shade will provide good side lighting to the face. A parchment or silk shade gives a soft side light, whereas a solid paper shade provides an up-and-downlight effect. If the inside of the shade is gold, the light reflected will be much warmer than if it is silver or white. Some old floor lamps may have up to three bulbs, two acting as downlights and one as an uplight by the addition of a simple white cone around it. Seen in some old houses, this is a good solution which is not often used today.

A combination of several lamps will help to create successful lighting. It is worthwhile introducing a lamp switch-line, so that lights can easily be switched on or off at the door, rather than at each lamp individually.

1 This miniature low-voltage downlight, used in a display cabinet, has an integral baffle to reduce the direct view of the bulb. This allows a focused beam of light to shine through the glass decanter and down onto the shelves beneath.

## Light bulbs (lamps)

There is a huge range of bulbs available, and some fixtures will require more specialized bulbs to achieve the desired effect. If this is the case, the manufacturer of the fixture will specify which bulb is required. The basic types of bulbs are described below, along with an indication of whether they are standard-voltage (operating at 120v) or low-voltage (operating at 12v and therefore requiring a transformer):

*A lamps [120v]*

These incandescent bulbs have a tungsten filament and are used mainly in table lamps, wall lights, and some hanging fixtures. They come in various shapes and sizes. In the United States, they always have a screw-in base; in some other countries they may have a "bayonet cap" base, which has two knobs which hook into the socket.

1 The pearl bulb, which has a milky-white appearance, gives a softer light than clear bulbs. If clear bulbs are used, for example, in a table lamp, patterns and shadows of the lampshade will be produced by the filament of the bulb on the ceiling, but when a pearl bulb is used these shadows will not occur.

2 Variations on the clear bulb include the half-chrome and silver bowl. These are useful when installed in low pendant fixtures over tables, as the light is reflected back into the shade, reducing direct glare. They can also be used in large parabolic spotlights, which have now largely been replaced by low-voltage fixtures.

"Bayonet" cap base

Screw-in base

*Candle lamps [120v]*

**3** These are incandescent bulbs molded into a pointed shape. Those made of clear glass are called torpedo bulbs. They are also available in pearlized glass and in twisted shapes for chandeliers. Once again, for small wall lights with shades, use pearl candle bulbs to avoid creating shadows; but in wall lights, lanterns, and chandeliers where the bare bulb is visible, use a clear torpedo bulb as the visible tungsten filament sparkles off the glass. Used with a dimmer, these bulbs emulate candlelight. Left undimmed, they can create glare.

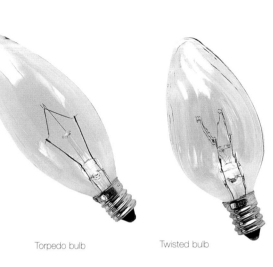

Torpedo bulb          Twisted bulb

**4** *Miniature candle lamps [120v] (not illustrated)*
These are primarily used in chandeliers, lanterns, and some wall lights where the appearance of a real candle is required. This small light source is far more elegant and creates less glare than a standard candle bulb and is the most suitable source where a visible bulb is required.

*Standard-voltage halogen lamps [120v]*
These bulbs have a long tungsten filament surrounded by halogen gas to make the light emitted much whiter.

**5** The single-ended version can replace standard A lamps, for example in a basement where a whiter light is required. These could be used in table lamps to give the room an instant lift and create a daylight effect.

**6** The double-ended variety is usually used in wall-mounted and free-standing halogen uplights, as well as exterior security floodlights.

*Reflector spotlights [120v]*

**7** ISL (internally silvered lamps and flood reflector lamps) are typically used in small standard-voltage downlights and spotlights, but the use of low-voltage and miniature standard-voltage bulbs is gradually limiting their use. Various wattages and sizes are available.

*Par 38 [120v]*

**8** This is the original standard-voltage spotlight, available in either incandescent or halogen. Its large size has meant that it has gradually been superseded by low-voltage halogen and smaller standard-voltage Par 20 lamps. It is now primarily used as a spotlight, particularly in gardens. Various wattages and sizes are available.

### Low-voltage halogen capsule [12v]

**9** This is a tiny compact bulb. Because it operates at a lower voltage, its filament has been reduced to a size that enables a small capsule to surround it. The grease from fingers can reduce its lamp life, and thus it should not be handled with bare hands. It can be used by itself in a fixture to create a starlight effect or with a reflector to focus the light emitted from the filament in a particular arrangement. Various wattages are available.

### Compact fluorescent [120v]

**10** These sources have miniaturized over the years and been reshaped as far as possible to match the A lamps, in both size and the lamp holder it fits into. They can therefore act as a direct energy-efficient swap; but care must be taken, as some of these bulbs are not dimmable.

### Low-voltage halogen dichroic reflector lamps [12v]

**11** This takes the small low-voltage capsule lamp and includes an integral dichroic reflector which focuses its light in a number of beam widths—narrow, medium, and flood. The dichroic nature of the reflector directs light forward and draws some heat back, creating a concentrated, slightly cooler beam of light. It is ideal for use in display lighting, and the flood versions of the lamp can be used in small fixtures for general downlighting. Various wattages are available operating at 12v. Two sizes are most common, 2 in. (5 cm.) diameter (MR16) and 1½ in. (4 cm.) diameter (MR11).

### Fiber optics (not illustrated)

These are increasingly becoming an important display lighting tool. They have been used for some time in museums because they cause no damage to valuable exhibits; although expensive, they have the major advantage of emitting no ultraviolet rays and no heat. Recent developments in both lenses and quality fiber-optic cable have helped make fiber optics more versatile. They are not a light source as such, but use either a metal halide or halogen source, which, with a special reflector, focuses at the end of a group of glass fibers sheathed in black; the light is transmitted down the glass fibers to be emitted at the end. The light source can therefore be remote, which can help maintenance.

*Fluorescent strips [120v]*

12 These have been developed into slimmer and smaller lengths. They can be used as uplights, uplighting from the top of a kitchen cabinet, for edge lighting, or for local task lighting, where a cool light source is required. They can be dimmed, but for this they require a special ballast.

*Incandescent tubes [120v]*

13 These are a tungsten filament alternative to fluorescent tubes. The light is softer but the lamp life is shorter, as the lamp filament is very fragile. The lamp is easily dimmable and can be used for soft uplighting effects. They can, for example, be used in areas where one part of a ceiling is raised and the light source can be concealed by a cornice, or they can be used as a soft under-counter light, or positioned on a mirror to provide side-lighting to the face.

*Mini track [12v]*

**14** This is a small, flexible track into which low-voltage bulbs can be set. The bulbs can be positioned at various intervals—every 2 in. (5 cm.), 4 in. (10 cm.), or possibly more. They use small low-voltage 3w, 5w, 8.5w, or 10w bulbs, and the transformers to feed these lamps need to be calculated accordingly. This type of fixture is ideal for display lighting in open shelves, cornice uplighting, or wherever a strip of light is required.

*Ropelight [120v and 12v]*

**15** This is a run of small "pea" lamps set into a flexible rubber covering. A simple standard-voltage ropelight is fairly small and has a long lamp life of 10,000 hours, approximately five years of normal use, after which the whole strip would need to be replaced. This is available in both low-voltage and standard-voltage versions, and is ideal for the soft delineation of features, whether creating a floating effect under a bed or lighting a bookshelf. This fixture has to be ordered to a precise size and is attached with a combination of double-sided tape and fixing clips.

# Glossary

**baffle** Device attached to a light fixture that helps to prevent glare. The source of light is set back behind the tube so that it is concealed from view.

**ballast** This is used to provide the correct start-up current for a fluorescent tube or compact. If a ballast is high frequency this means the bulb is switched on immediately and avoids the flicker. If a fluorescent is to be dimmed it is necessary to ensure that the ballast is dimmable (usually they are not) and specify this.

**bollard lights** Low-level post light which has a similar purpose to a path light but is tougher and more sturdy than the path light. Often used in commercial situations.

**cable system** Type of track with two tensioned cables, powered at 12v, carrying the current to small low-voltage fixtures placed between the cables.

**cornice board** The baffle usually built below a cabinet to conceal a light source.

**cross lighting** Way of accenting a picture, plant, or ornament by lighting it from two different directions so that the beams of light overlap on the object.

**dichroic lamp (MR type)** Bulb that has a reflector designed to pass the majority of its heat output backward, in the opposite direction to the beam of light.

**directional source** Light fitting that casts light in a specific direction; usually mounted or recessed into the ceiling, they can be tilted for extra adaptability.

**discharge sources** Low-energy, high-output light source, e.g. metal halide and sodium, which has a few seconds start-up time. Used mainly in street lighting and stadiums.

**door-operated switch** Switch set inside a door of a piece of furniture (mainly closets and refrigerators) which automatically turns the light on when the door is opened.

**drum-shaped uplights** Compact low-intensity uplight, intended primarily for feature lighting. Often used under plants or in the corners of rooms.

**electrical outlet** Device into which an electrical plug can be inserted in order to make a connection in a switchline.

**extendible bracket** Bracket made with two or three sections that can either be folded back on itself or extended to provide a long arm.

**filament** Thin wire (usually tungsten) inside a light bulb that heats up to provide light.

**flexi-arm** Adjustable arm, usually composed of metal links, which can be adjusted to light in almost any direction. Ideal when used for a task light.

**illuminator** Used for fiber optics, the light source is within a box where a reflector focuses the light to the end of the glass fibers.

**lamp beam width** Measure of the spread of illumination obtained from a reflector as part of a bulb or fixture [narrow 14°, medium 27° or wide 40°].

**lenses** Accessories used to achieve different effects from the same fixture.

>**spread lens** Accessory used to achieve an elongated beam of light when used in conjunction with a narrow-beam bulb.

>**frosted lens** Accessory used to achieve a more even wash of light.

**metal reflector lamp** Bulb that has a solid reflector to direct light and heat forward (unlike a dichroic lamp which sends some of the heat backward).

**"moonlighting"** Technique used in exterior lighting where the lights are installed at high level in a tree to filter down through the leaves to create a "moonlight" effect.

**path light** Usually mounted on a stem, this fixture has a bulb positioned underneath a "hat" or top which reflects the light down onto the path, e.g. "mushroom" type.

**projecting the light (pictures)** Low-voltage fixture which is specially designed for accent lighting; it has a system of lenses and shutters that can shape the light beam to the exact outline of the picture or object being lit.

**recessed fixture** Very discreet fixture that can be positioned within the ceiling, floor, or wall, flush with the level of the surface, instead of being mounted on top of the surface.

**reflector** This can form part of a bulb or a fixture and is used to direct light in a specific beam. Reflectors can be designed to provide either a narrow or wide distribution of light.

**shuttering devices (barn door attachments etc.)** Metal attachments on a fixture which help to control the spread of light.

**stem-mounted lights** Variety of outdoor fixtures which come with a stem to be inserted into the ground; this makes the positioning of the fixtures are very flexible.

**switchline** Here it is used to mean the various fittings which are connected to one switch or dimmer, i.e. all fittings on one switchline operate together at the same level.

**transformer** Device that reduces the domestic electricity supply from standard voltage to the required low voltage.

**UV (ultraviolet)** Part of the electromagnetic spectrum. Can be harmful to artwork: lenses are available to help reduce these rays.

# Suppliers

### Ace Hardware
Rockland
California
T: (916) 632-2200 call for store locations
- *Bulbs*

### Aretmide
Farmingdale
New York
T: (516) 694-9292 call for catalog and distributor
- *Contemporary lighting*

### City Lights
San Francisco
California
T: (415) 863-2020
- *Bulbs, contemporary and classic lighting*

### Counter Clockwise
Jasper
Alberta
T: (403) 852-3152
- *Contemporary lighting*

### Crate & Barrell
T: (800) 606-6387 call for store locations
www.crateandbarrel.com
- *Contemporary lighting*

### D'ac Lighting Inc.
Mamaroneck
New York
T: (914) 698-5959
- *Contemporary lighting*

### Domicile
Calgary
Alberta
T: (403) 261-6044
- *Contemporary lighting*

### Flos USA
T: (800) 939-3567 call for distributors
- *Contemporary lighting*

### GE Lighting
T: (800) GE-LAMPS call for distributors
www.gespectrum.com
- *Bulbs*

### George Kovacs Lighting
Long Island City
New York
T: (718) 392-8190
- *Contemporary lighting*

### Home Depot
T: (800) 430-3376 call for store locations
www.homedepot.com
- *Contemporary lighting*

### Ikea
T: (800) 959-3349 call for store locations
www.ikea.com
- *Contemporary lighting*

### International Association of Lighting Designers
New York
New York
T: (212) 206-1281 call for information about lighting design

### Just Shades
T: (212) 966-2757
- *Shades of all shapes and types*

### Kichler Lighting
Cleveland
Ohio
T: (216) 573 1000 call for distributors
- *Catalog available for traditional and garden fixtures*

### Koch & Lowy
Avon
Massachusetts
T: (508) 588-4700 call for distributors
- *Contemporary and classic lighting*

### Lamps Plus
T: (800) 300-7721 call for store locations
- *Contemporary and classic lighting*

### Leucos Lighting
Edison
New Jersey
T: (908) 225-0010 call for distributors
- *Contemporary lighting*

### Lightolier
T: (800) 215-1068 call for distributors
- *Contemporary and classic lighting*

### Limn Company
San Francisco
California
T: (415) 543-5466
www.limn.com
- *Contemporary and classic lighting*

## Luceplan

New York
New York
T: (800) 268-7790
• *Contemporary lighting*

## Luxo Lamp Corp

Port Chester
New York
T: (800) 222-LUXO call for distributors
• *Contemporary lighting*

## Melusina

Calgary
Alberta
T: (403) 261-9780
• *Contemporary lighting*

## Nationwide Light Sources

Virginia Beach
Virginia
T: (800) 882 8834
or (757) 424 8636 in Virginia
F: (757) 424 6186
lightsources@earthlink.net
www.lightsourcesinc.com

## Orchard Supply Hardware

T: (888) SHOP-OSH call for store locations
www.osh.com
• *Bulbs, contemporary lighting*

## Pottery Barn

T: (800) 922-5507 call for store locations
www.potterybarn.com
• *Contemporary lighting*

## Rejuvenation Lamp and Fixture

Portland
Oregon
T: (503) 231-1900
• *Classic lighting*

## Renovator's Supply

Conway
New Hampshire
T: (800) 659-2211
• *Classic lighting*

## Restoration Hardware

T: (800) 762-1005
www.restorationhardware.com
• *Contemporary and classic lighting*

## Sears

T: (800) 972-4687 call for store locations
www.sears.com
• *Contemporary lighting*

## Sescolite Lighting Centres

Toronto
Ontario
T: (416) 651-6570

## Sylvania

T: (800) 544-4828 call for distributors
www.sylvania.com
• *Bulbs*

## Union Electric Lighting Co.

Toronto
Ontario
T: (416) 652-2200
• *Contemporary lighting*

# Index

Figures in italics refer to captions.

# Author's acknowledgments

Many thanks to Sarah Roberts, Elaine Parker, Marie Claire Haselden and Christopher Fordham for all their invaluable help and advice.

# Publisher's acknowledgments

The publisher would like to thank stylist Arabella McNie for her work on the dining table project on pages 44–5 and Dusti Helms of Thompson & Sears Lighting Design in New York. Many thanks to all those who allowed their homes and gardens to be photographed. Thanks also to those who gave permission for their photographs to appear in this book: 1 VNU/Hans Zeegers/*Living;* 2 Ray Main/ Mainstream; 5 Tom Stewart/lighting design by John Cullen Lighting; 6 Tom Stewart; 8 *World of Interiors*/Annabel Elston/lighting design David Gill; 9 above Undine Pröhl; 9 below Ray Main/Mainstream; 10 Lars Hallen/Design Press; 11 left Robert Harding Picture Library/James Merrell/© IPC Magazines Ltd/*Homes & Gardens*/ lighting design by John Cullen Lighting; 11 right Axiom/James Morris/architect Claudio Silvestrin; 12 above Ian McKinnell; 12 below View/Peter Cook/Woolf Architects; 14 Axiom/James Morris/lighting design by John Cullen Lighting/interior design by Lassman Interiors; 15 Axiom/James Morris; 16 Arcaid/Richard Bryant/ Paxton Locher Architects; 16-17 View/Chris Gascoigne/architect Norman Foster; 19 above left Ray Main/Mainstream/Yeoward; 19 above right Camera Press/ *Schöner Wohnen;* 19 below David Spero/architect Seth Stein; 20 View/Chris Gascoigne/architect Seth Stein; 22 Axiom/James Morris/architect Will White; 23 Marianne Majerus; 24 Tom Stewart/lighting design by John Cullen Lighting/ architecture and interior design by Oliver Morgan Architects; 25 above left & above right Tom Stewart; 25 above centre Tom Stewart/lighting design by John Cullen Lighting/interior design by Reed Creative; 25 below Ken Hayden/interior design by Reed Creative; 26 left The Interior Archive/Fritz von der Schulenburg/ architect Jean Oh; 26 right Ray Main/Mainstream/designer Llewelyn-Bowen; 27 Tim Street-Porter/Designer Brian Murphy; 28 left Tom Stewart/lighting design by John Cullen Lighting/architecture and interior design by Oliver Morgan Associates; 28 right Fritz von der Schulenburg/*House & Garden*/© The Condé Nast Publications Ltd/interior design by Lassman Interiors; 29 left Deidi von Schaewen; 29 right Ray Main/Mainstream; 30 Tom Stewart/lighting design by John Cullen Lighting/architecture and interior design by Oliver Morgan Architects; 31 left Tom Stewart/lighting design by John Cullen Lighting; 31 right Elizabeth Whiting & Associates/Michael Dunne; 32-33 Michael Moran/Moneo Brock Architects; 34-35 Ken Hayden/lighting design by John Cullen Lighting/interior design by Reed Creative; 36-37 Tom Stewart/lighting design by John Cullen Lighting; 38-39 Richard Glover/architect John Pawson; 39 above Ray Main/ Mainstream; 39 below Ray Main/Mainstream; 40 Ray Main/Mainstream; 41 *World of Interiors*/Henry Bourne; 42-43 Tom Stewart/lighting design by John Cullen Lighting; 44-45 Tom Stewart/lighting design by John Cullen Lighting/architecture and interior design by Oliver Morgan Architects/Soft Furnishing by Reed Creative; 46-47 Tom Stewart/lighting design by John Cullen Lighting/interior design by Lassman Interiors; 48 Axiom/James Morris; 49 Elizabeth Whiting & Associates; 50-51 Axiom/James Morris/lighting design by John Cullen Lighting/architecture and interior design by Littman Goddard Hogarth; 52 left Christophe Demonfaucon/ architect François Roche; 52 right Ray Main/Mainstream; 53 Axiom/James Morris/ architect James Gorst; 54 above Axiom/James Morris/architect Will White; 54 below Tom Stewart/lighting design by John Cullen Lighting/interior Design by Reed Creative; 55 left Ken Hayden/lighting design by John Cullen Lighting/interior design by Reed Creative; 55 right View/Dennis Gilbert; 56-57 Axiom/James Morris/lighting design by John Cullen Lighting/interior design by Tim Boyd and Alex Michaelis Associates; 57 Tom Stewart/lighting design by John Cullen Lighting/interior design by Tim Boyd and Alex Michaelis Associates; 58 View/ Chris Gascoigne/architect Seth Stein; 59 Axiom/James Morris; 60-61 The Interior Archive/Fritz von der Schulenburg/lighting design by John Cullen Lighting/interior design Todhunter Earle; 62 Axiom/James Morris/architect John Pawson; 63 *World of Interiors*/Annabel Elston; 64 Axiom/James Morris/architect John Pardey; 65 above © One Aldwych, London/lighting design by Lighting Design International/ interior design by Mary Fox Linton; 65 below The Interior Archive/ Andrew Wood/designer Spencer Fung; 66 View/Dennis Gilbert/architect Rick Mather; 67 View/Chris Gascoigne; 68 left Ray Main/Mainstream; 68 right View/ Dennis Gilbert/architect Bernhard Blauel; 69 Ken Hayden/lighting design by John Cullen Lighting/interior design by Reed Creative; 70 Paul Ryan/ International Interiors/architects Pierce & Allen; 71 Axiom/James Morris; 72 Arcaid/Earl Carter/ Belle/architect Grey Anderson; 73 Tom Stewart; 74-75 Ken Hayden/interior design by Reed Creative; 76 *Marie Claire Maison*/ Gilles de Chabaneix/Catherine Ardouin; 77 left Ray Main/Mainstream; 77 right *Marie Claire Maison*/Nicolas Tosni/J Borgeaud; 78 Christian Sarramon; 79 Marianne Majerus/lighting effect designed by George Carter; 80 View/Peter Cook; 80-81 Axiom/James Morris/lighting design by John Cullen Lighting/garden design by R K Alliston; 81 Marianne Majerus/lighting effect designed by George Carter; 82-83 Tom Stewart/lighting design by John Cullen Lighting/garden design by Arne Maynard; 84 Camera Press/*Schöner Wohnen;* 85 Tom Stewart/lighting design by John Cullen Lighting/ Garden Design by Arne Maynard; 86 Ray Main/Mainstream; 89 Axiom/James Morris; 91 Tom Stewart; 92-97 Patrick McLeavy; 99 Tom Stewart.